Cats Wearing Clothes

A Photo Journey Through the Ages

S.C. Francis

Into The Unknown
Publishing

Contents

Dedicated to Meow Meow

PREHISTORIC ERA

The Beginning

In the vast and mysterious expanse of prehistory, before the ink of recorded history touched the pages of human existence, our ancient ancestors danced to the rhythm of life in a world untouched by the convenience we enjoy today. Let's embark on a brief journey through this extraordinary era, filled with important events that have shaped our species.

Life in the Wild:
In the Paleolithic Era, our precursors navigated life with stone tools, and their fashion sense consisted of animal hides and the occasional leafy accessory. Survival was the name of the game, and our ancestors roamed as nomadic hunter-gatherers, foraging for food and hunting woolly mammoths.

A Quest for Fire:
One of the most critical achievements of this time was mastering the art of fire. Picture this: darkness falls, and there's a chilly wind, but you've got a crackling fire, providing warmth, light, and a sense of security. This was the era when humans became the ultimate pyromaniacs and, in doing so, took a monumental leap forward.

The Agricultural Revolution:
Fast forward to the Neolithic Era, and a radical change is afoot. Our ancestors decided they'd had enough of wandering and discovered farming. They stopped chasing herds of animals and started cultivating their own crops. This agricultural shift signaled the beginning of a more settled life, as our species began building permanent communities and honing the art of agriculture.

The Birth of Civilization:
These settlements evolved into early civilizations, such as the Sumerians and Egyptians, where the alphabet was invented, pyramids were built, and pharaohs ruled. Imagine the first scribbles of cuneiform on clay tablets, laying the groundwork for the stories, poetry, and memes of the future.

Monumental Achievements:
From Stonehenge in England to the Great Pyramids of Giza, prehistoric people left their mark on the world in the form of magnificent monuments. These awe-inspiring structures still stand today, leaving us to marvel at the intelligence and determination of our ancestors.

ANCIENT EGYPT

Ancient Egypt

Travel back in time to the cradle of civilization, along the fertile banks of the mighty Nile River, where one of the world's most fascinating civilizations blossomed - Ancient Egypt. This enchanting realm, steeped in grandeur, mysticism, and timeless allure, has captured the imaginations of generations and continues to unfold its secrets.

Life Along the Nile:
At the heart of Ancient Egypt lay the Nile River, a lifeline that offered sustenance, prosperity, and spiritual significance. Its annual floods turned the desert into a lush oasis, providing the resources that allowed this civilization to flourish. The Nile wasn't just a river; it was revered as a benevolent deity, the giver of life itself.

Pharaohs and Pyramids:
The pharaohs, god-kings who ruled with divine authority, held the keys to this civilization's grandeur. Their reigns were marked by majestic ceremonies, vast construction projects, and towering monuments. The iconic pyramids, the eternal resting places of these rulers, are architectural marvels that continue to astound. The Great Pyramid of Giza, the last remaining wonder of the ancient world, is a testament to the astonishing architectural achievements of the era.

Hieroglyphic Enigma:
In this world, language was a work of art. Hieroglyphics, the intricate script of symbols, adorned tombs, temples, and artifacts. Each symbol was not just a word; it was a picture, a story, and a bridge to the past. Hieroglyphics were more than words; they were the thread that wove the tapestry of ancient Egyptian culture, capturing their history, spirituality, and wisdom.

Elegant Attire:
Fashion in Ancient Egypt was not just clothing; it was a reflection of identity and social status. Linen robes, woven from fine threads, were the attire of choice. The whites of their garments symbolized purity, and the garments were comfortable in the desert climate. In a civilization that reveled in vibrant colors, the elite adorned themselves with intricately patterned and colorful garments. Their love for jewelry knew no bounds; from rings to bracelets, necklaces to earrings, the accessories weren't just ornamental; they were status symbols, tangible representations of wealth and prestige.

Mummies and the Beyond:
One of the most captivating aspects of Ancient Egypt is their profound belief in the afterlife. This belief led to the development of the intricate and revered practice of mummification, an art that preserved the body for the journey to eternity. Tombs, filled with treasures, sustenance, and protective spells, showcased the faith in an opulent afterlife.

Cosmic Connection:
In the heart of this civilization, priests were more than spiritual guides; they were astronomers and mathematicians, charting the heavens with meticulous precision. They believed in a profound connection between the earthly realm and the cosmic order, aligning temples and pyramids with the celestial bodies above.

CLASSICAL GREECE

Classical Greece

Step into a world where marble statues come to life, where philosophy blossoms, and where the foundations of democracy are laid - welcome to Classical Greece. This enchanting epoch, spanning from the 5th to the 4th century BC, was a cradle of intellectual and artistic achievements, and it continues to shape our modern world.

Birth of Democracy:
The very essence of democracy, a system of governance that empowers the citizens, was nurtured in Classical Greece. In the Athenian city-state, a direct democracy was established, allowing every eligible citizen a voice in decision-making. Meetings in the Agora, the bustling marketplace, were arenas for political discourse and debate.

Philosophical Giants:
Classical Greece was a hotbed of philosophical thought, with luminaries like Socrates, Plato, and Aristotle. Socrates' method of questioning, still known as the Socratic method, encouraged critical thinking. Plato's Academy was one of the first institutions of higher learning, and his writings laid the groundwork for Western philosophy. Aristotle, a polymath, delved into areas from ethics to biology, leaving an indelible mark on our understanding of the world.

Olympian Artistry:
The art of Classical Greece was a marvel of elegance and precision. Sculptors like Phidias crafted the iconic statues of gods and heroes, each bearing an astonishingly lifelike quality. The Parthenon, a temple dedicated to the goddess Athena, was adorned with sculptures and friezes that have become symbols of classical artistry. The Greeks also introduced theater, giving birth to the tragedies and comedies that continue to influence dramatic storytelling.

Epic Epics:
Homer's epic poems, the "Iliad" and the "Odyssey," became cornerstones of Western literature. These masterpieces are not only tales of heroism but also examinations of human nature, morality, and the human condition.

The Spirit of Competition:
The Greeks embraced the spirit of competition and physical excellence with the Olympic Games. Held every four years in Olympia, these contests featured athletic feats and served as a platform for city-states to showcase their prowess and unity.

Mythology and Religion:
The Greek pantheon, with gods like Zeus, Athena, and Apollo, was an integral part of life. Temples and rituals celebrated the divine, and mythology was woven into the fabric of Greek culture.

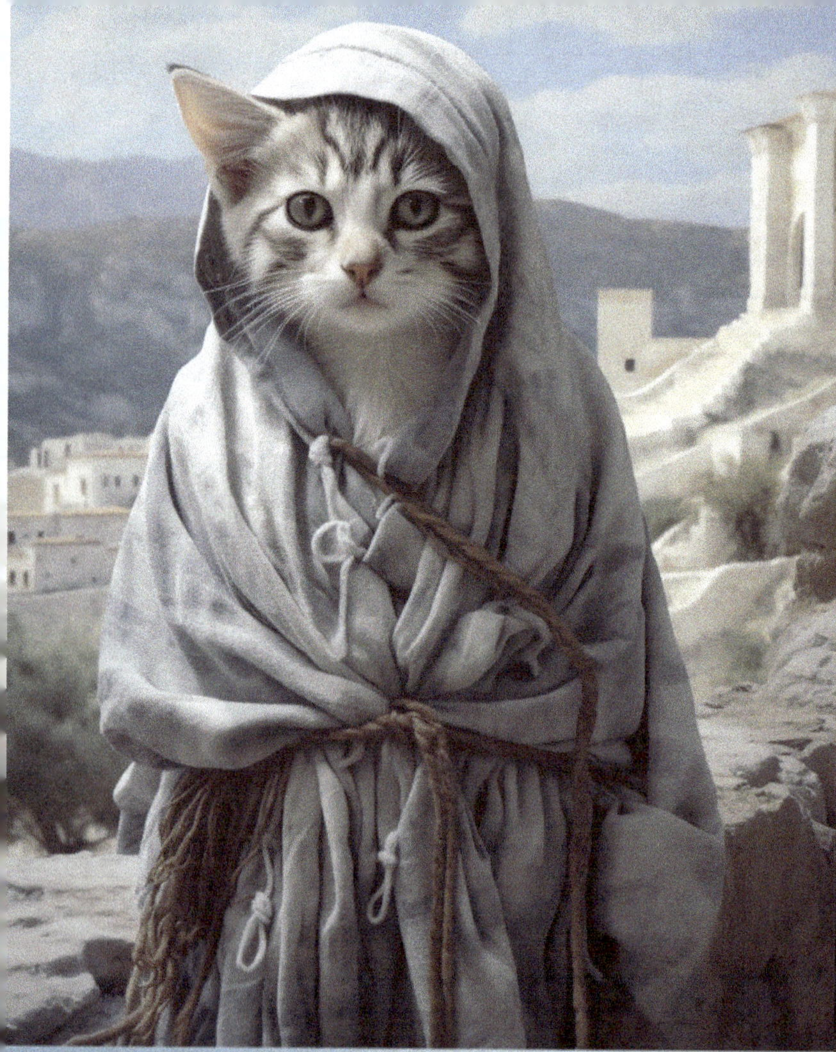
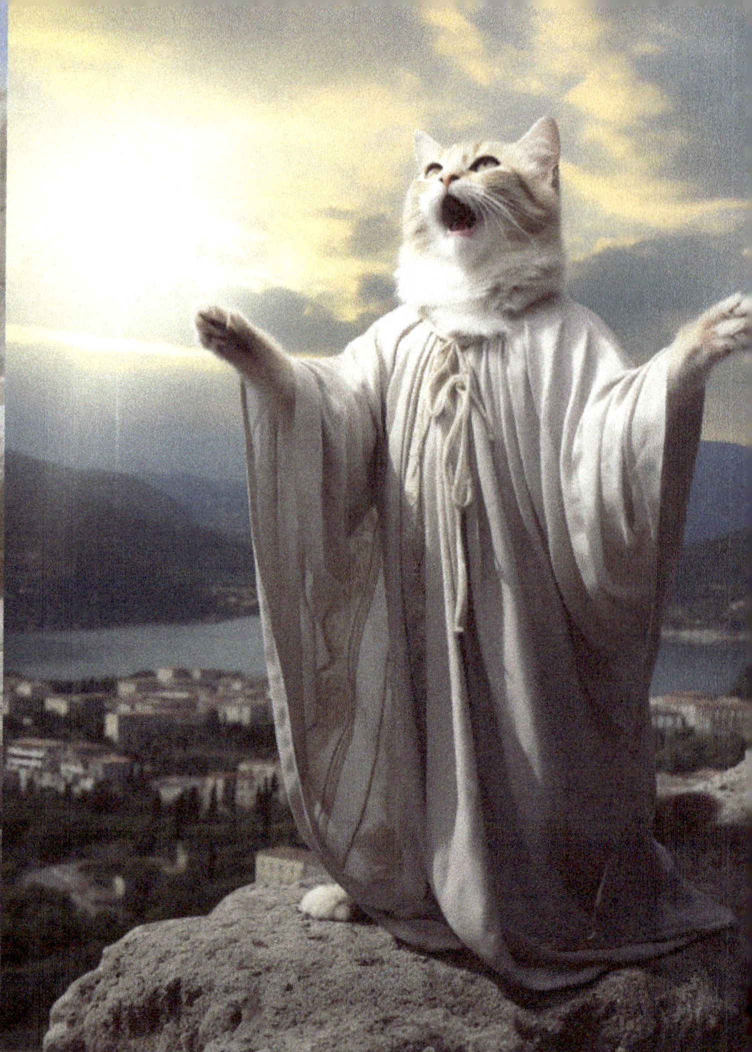
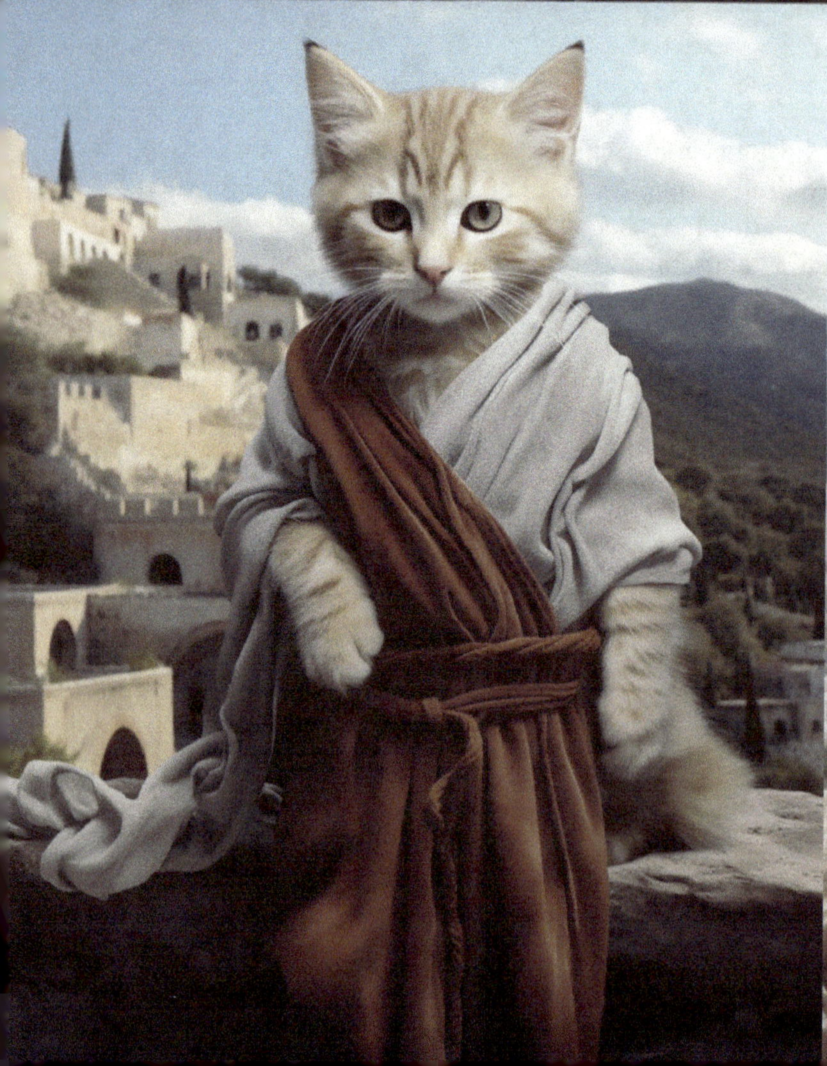
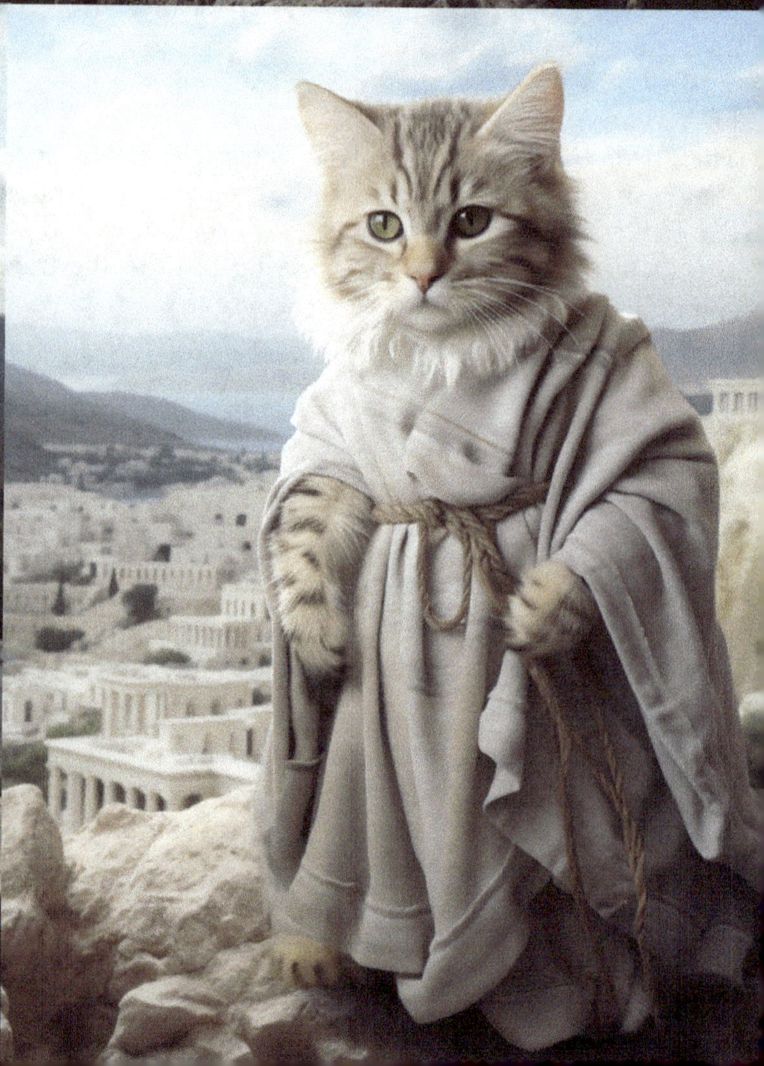

ROMAN EMPIRE

Roman Empire

Enter the sprawling dominion of the Roman Empire, a realm of military might, architectural marvels, and cultural riches that spanned over a millennium. From the legendary foundation of Rome in 753 BC to the fall of the Western Roman Empire in 476 AD, this fascinating empire has left an indelible mark on history and continues to captivate the world with its tales of power and glory.

The Rise of Rome:
It all began as a humble city on the banks of the Tiber River. Rome's legendary founding story involving Romulus and Remus, twin brothers raised by a she-wolf, is as enchanting as it is mythical. Over the centuries, Rome expanded, and its unyielding military prowess allowed it to conquer and unify the Italian Peninsula.

Masters of Warfare:
The legions of Rome were an awe-inspiring force, characterized by discipline, tactics, and engineering. Their well-trained soldiers, equipped with the short sword gladii and the throwing spear pilum, expanded the Roman borders to create one of the largest empires in the world.

Architectural Marvels:
The Romans were not just warriors; they were master builders. The Colosseum, an iconic amphitheater that could hold over 50,000 spectators, hosted gladiatorial contests and chariot races, captivating audiences with grand spectacles. The Pantheon, a marvel of engineering, still stands as a testament to Roman ingenuity.

Roman Law and Governance:
The Romans were pioneers of law and governance. Their legal system, embodied in the Twelve Tables, was a foundation for modern legal codes. The Roman Senate, with its rich history, served as a model for representative governance.

Cultural Riches:
The Romans revered culture, literature, and art. Writers like Virgil penned the epic "Aeneid," while poets like Ovid and Horace celebrated love and nature. Roman artists created stunning mosaics and frescoes, and they brought lifelike statues and portraits to life.

Religion and Mythology:
The Romans blended their deities with those of the Greeks, creating a rich pantheon. Jupiter, Mars, Venus, and Neptune were just a few of the gods and goddesses they worshipped. The architectural wonders of the Temple of Jupiter Optimus Maximus and the Temple of Saturn bore testament to their devotion.

The Fall of an Empire:
The Western Roman Empire eventually succumbed to internal strife, economic decline, and external pressures. In 476 AD, the Germanic chieftain Odoacer deposed the last Roman emperor, Romulus Augustulus, marking the end of a once-mighty empire.

MEDIEVAL EUROPE

Medieval Europe

C ome into the mystical world of Medieval Europe, where the clank of armor resonated through towering castles, and tales of heroic knights and courtly love captivated hearts and minds. This fascinating era, roughly spanning from the 5th to the 15th century, was a time of both darkness and illumination, where the echoes of the past met the dawn of the modern age.

The Medieval Tapestry:
The term "medieval" often conjures images of knights in shining armor, and while this is undoubtedly a part of the story, the era was a complex tapestry of political turmoil, cultural transformation, and religious devotion. The medieval world comprised kingdoms and fiefdoms, each with its own set of laws and rulers. Feudalism, a hierarchical system, determined the relationships between lords, vassals, and serfs.

The Castle Strongholds:
Medieval Europe was marked by the omnipresent castle, both a symbol of power and a fortress of defense. Castles were epic edifices of stone, towering over the landscape, offering protection and grandeur to their lords. These strongholds often featured intricate mazes of chambers, grand halls, and imposing battlements.

Knighthood and Chivalry:
The knight, a central figure in medieval society, was a mounted and armored warrior who swore fealty to a lord in exchange for land. Chivalry, a code of conduct rooted in courage, loyalty, and respect, guided the actions of knights. They were the protectors of their lords and the realm, and their gallant deeds inspired tales of heroism and courtly love.

The Silk Road and Beyond:
Medieval Europe was not an isolated world; it was part of a larger global tapestry. The Silk Road, an ancient trade network connecting Europe to Asia, brought exotic goods, ideas, and cultures to the continent. The Crusades, a series of religious and military expeditions, sought to reclaim the Holy Land from Muslim rule and fostered cultural exchange between East and West.

Religion and the Church:
The medieval era was a time of deep religious faith, with the Catholic Church serving as a spiritual and political power. Cathedrals, such as Chartres and Notre-Dame, were awe-inspiring examples of medieval architecture. Monasteries were centers of learning and preservation, where manuscripts and knowledge were safeguarded.

The Renaissance Dawn:
As the medieval period drew to a close, the seeds of the Renaissance, an era of renewed interest in art, science, and exploration, began to take root. The medieval world gave way to a new age of enlightenment and progress, but its legacy continued to influence the unfolding drama of history.

RENAISSANCE

Renaissance

The Renaissance, a period of profound transformation and intellectual fervor, emerges as one of the most vibrant and dynamic epochs in human history. Spanning roughly from the 14th to the 17th century, it was a time when the darkness of the Middle Ages gave way to a brilliant burst of creativity, culminating in an explosion of art, science, and human exploration.

The Seeds of Change:
The Renaissance's roots can be traced back to the late Middle Ages, as the vestiges of feudalism and religious dogma began to crumble. The human spirit sought to soar beyond the confinements of the past, and the Renaissance became the platform for this ambitious ascent.

Artistic Resplendence:
Art was at the heart of the Renaissance, with Italy as its epicenter. Masters like Leonardo da Vinci, Michelangelo, and Raphael created exquisite works of art, such as the Mona Lisa and the ceiling of the Sistine Chapel. Their artistry captured the human form and spirit with an unprecedented level of detail and depth, echoing the values of the age.

Scientific Enlightenment:
The Renaissance was not just about art; it was an age of scientific awakening. Pioneers like Galileo Galilei and Johannes Kepler challenged traditional beliefs and laid the foundation for modern science. Galileo's telescopic observations of the cosmos revolutionized our understanding of the universe.

Humanism and the Printing Press:
Humanism, a scholarly movement that celebrated human potential and classical learning, was a driving force. The printing press, invented by Johannes Gutenberg, played a pivotal role in the dissemination of knowledge. It made books more accessible, paving the way for the widespread circulation of ideas and intellectual exchange.

Exploration and Discovery:
The Renaissance was also a time of exploration and adventure. Christopher Columbus's journey to the New World in 1492 marked the beginning of an age of exploration that would reshape the known world and redefine cultural boundaries. Vasco da Gama, Ferdinand Magellan, and other explorers opened up new frontiers, connecting the far reaches of the globe.

From Darkness to Light:
The Renaissance was a transition from the dimly lit medieval chambers of the past to the brilliant illumination of a new era. It was a time of transition, transformation, and triumph. The human spirit flourished, and the seeds planted during this age of enlightenment continue to bear fruit, shaping the course of human history to this day.

BAROQUE

Baroque

Enter the opulent world of the Baroque Period, a time when art, music, and architecture swirled together in a grand spectacle of extravagance and emotion. Spanning roughly from the early 17th to the mid-18th century, the Baroque era was a dramatic departure from the Renaissance's restraint, marked by bold expression, vibrant creativity, and an unapologetic celebration of the senses.

The Theatrical Flourish:
The term "Baroque" itself conjures the dramatic, and that's precisely what this period was all about. In stark contrast to the order and balance of the Renaissance, Baroque art and architecture aimed to astonish and overwhelm. This was an era of theatrics, where every work of art and every building was a stage set for a grand performance.

Ornate Architecture:
In architecture, the Baroque period gave us extravagant churches and palaces. One of the most iconic examples is the Palace of Versailles in France, a testament to the extravagance of the age. Its Hall of Mirrors, adorned with intricate gilded ornamentation and hundreds of mirrors, remains a symbol of opulence.

Exquisite Music:
The Baroque era produced some of the most enduring music in history. Composers like Johann Sebastian Bach, George Frideric Handel, and Antonio Vivaldi crafted works that celebrated the fusion of melody and emotion. Bach's intricate fugues, Handel's powerful oratorios, and Vivaldi's evocative concertos are still cherished today.

Opera's Sensory Delight:
Opera emerged as a prominent art form during the Baroque period. The work of Claudio Monteverdi and Henry Purcell showcased the power of music, drama, and singing combined. Ornate sets, elaborate costumes, and intense emotion made opera an immersive experience.

Sculptural Marvels:
Baroque sculpture was characterized by dynamic forms and elaborate detail. Gian Lorenzo Bernini, one of the most influential sculptors of the era, created masterpieces like "Apollo and Daphne" and "The Ecstasy of Saint Teresa," where marble seemed to come alive in breathtaking narratives.

The Baroque Legacy:
The Baroque era was a bridge between the Renaissance and the Enlightenment, leaving an indelible mark on art, music, and culture. It was an era of vitality, with its exuberance, emotional intensity, and artistic flourish echoing through the centuries.

VICTORIAN ERA

Victorian Era

Behold the radiant world of the Victorian Era, a time of unparalleled elegance, social transformation, and the cradle of the Industrial Revolution. Spanning from 1837 to 1901 during the reign of Queen Victoria of England, this remarkable period is characterized by its paradoxical blend of luxury and societal progress.

The Long and Enduring Reign:
Queen Victoria's rule, the 2nd longest in British history, stretched for over six decades, leaving an indelible mark on the era that bears her name. Her reign saw the British Empire expand to its zenith, spanning a quarter of the world's landmass.

Industrial Revolution Unleashed:
The Victorian Era was an age of rapid industrialization. Factories powered by steam engines, transformed production and transportation. Railways crisscrossed the nation, facilitating the movement of goods and people. This period witnessed profound technological and economic shifts, with innovations like the telegraph and the spread of electric power.

Elegant Fashion:
Victorian fashion was a sight to behold. Women's dresses were characterized by their opulent layers, with voluminous skirts and bodices that cinched at the waist. Men, on the other hand, sported tailored suits, top hats, and cravats. The era also saw the emergence of mourning attire, with black attire and mourning jewelry reflecting the period's obsession with death and mourning rituals.

Intricate Decor and Design:
The Victorian home was a sanctuary of elaborate decor. Ornate furniture, heavy drapery, and rich color palettes were hallmarks of Victorian interior design. The Gothic Revival and Renaissance Revival styles had a profound influence on architecture, and homes were adorned with turrets, pointed arches, and intricate ornamentation.

Scientific Advancements:
The Victorian Era was also a time of groundbreaking scientific discovery. Charles Darwin's theory of evolution, detailed in "On the Origin of Species," revolutionized biology. Florence Nightingale pioneered modern nursing, and her work in healthcare reform laid the foundation for contemporary nursing practices.

The Social Quilt:
Victorian society was characterized by strict social hierarchies. The upper class reveled in opulence, while the working class toiled under challenging conditions. The period also witnessed significant social reforms, such as the abolition of slavery and movements for women's rights.

A Legacy of Dichotomy:
The Victorian Era's legacy is one of paradox, where the extravagance of the upper classes clashed with the harsh realities of the lower classes. It was an age of transformation, marked by profound shifts in technology, culture, and society, setting the stage for the modern world.

1900S

1900s Decade

The turn of the 20th century brought the world into a new era filled with hope, innovation, and a sense of boundless possibilities. The decade from 1900 to 1910 witnessed profound changes in technology, culture, and society, setting the stage for the modern age.

Dawning of a New Century:
As the 20th century dawned, there was a palpable sense of optimism and anticipation. The world had survived the uncertainties of the 19th century, including the Industrial Revolution and widespread political upheaval. People were eager to embrace the promises of a new century, marked by the possibilities of scientific discovery and progress.

Technological Marvels:
The early 1900s were a time of rapid technological advancement. In 1903, the Wright brothers achieved the first powered flight, and their achievement opened the skies to new possibilities. The era also saw the development of the Ford Model T in 1908, making automobiles more accessible to the masses.

The Telegraph and Communication:
Communication was rapidly evolving. In 1901, the first transatlantic wireless transmission by Marconi connected distant shores. This was an era when letters, telegrams, and the burgeoning field of journalism were the primary means of staying informed and connected.

Fashion and Culture:
The fashion of the early 1900s was marked by a transition from the elaborate, corseted styles of the late 19th century to a more relaxed, Edwardian silhouette. Women's dresses featured high necklines, long skirts, and intricate lace, while men's attire still included formal suits, top hats, and cravats.

Innovations in Entertainment:
The early 1900s were a time of exciting developments in entertainment. The film industry was in its infancy, with silent movies capturing the public's imagination. The first feature film, "The Great Train Robbery," was released in 1903.

Scientific Advancements:
In the realm of science, this period was marked by significant discoveries. Marie Curie's groundbreaking research on radioactivity led to her receiving Nobel Prizes in both physics and chemistry. Albert Einstein, in 1905, published his theory of special relativity, a groundbreaking development in the understanding of the physical universe.

The World in Flux:
The early 1900s were an era of transition, poised between the grandeur of the 19th century and the tumultuous changes of the 20th century. It was a time when the world was awakening to new possibilities, propelled by the power of innovation and human ingenuity.

1910S

1910s Decade

The 1910s, often overshadowed by the turbulence of World War I and the grandeur of the Roaring Twenties, was a decade of profound change and transition. It was a time when the world was on the cusp of modernity, and the echoes of the past still reverberated in society, politics, and culture.

A World on the Verge of War:
As the decade began, the world was teetering on the precipice of war. Europe's great powers were entangled in a web of political alliances and rivalries. The assassination of Archduke Franz Ferdinand of Austria-Hungary in 1914 ignited the flames of World War I, setting the stage for a global conflict of unprecedented scale and devastation.

Technological Advancements:
The 1910s were marked by significant technological advancements. Innovations in communication, including the transatlantic wireless transmission and the first commercial transatlantic flight, were transforming the world.

Women's Suffrage:
Women's suffrage movements gained momentum during the 1910s. Women across the globe were advocating for the right to vote and participate in civic life. In the United States, suffragettes like Alice Paul and Lucy Burns fought for women's rights, eventually leading to the ratification of the 19th Amendment in 1920.

The Titanic and Tragedy:
The sinking of the RMS Titanic in 1912 was a poignant symbol of human ambition and tragedy. The ship, touted as "unsinkable," met its tragic end in the North Atlantic, claiming more than 1,500 lives and serving as a reminder of the perils of hubris.

The Great War and the Redrawing of Maps:
World War I, with its trench warfare and devastating battles, brought unprecedented destruction. The war redrew the map of Europe, leading to the dissolution of empires and the creation of new nations. The Treaty of Versailles, which ended the conflict in 1919, sought to establish peace but sowed the seeds of future discord.

A Transition to Modernity:
The 1910s was a bridge between the 19th and 20th centuries. It was a decade of transition, marked by the lingering vestiges of a bygone era and the inexorable march toward modernity. The cataclysm of World War I and the innovations of the age set the stage for the transformative decades that would follow.

Legacy and Remembrance:
The 1910s were a time of change, challenge, and transition. It was a decade when the world grappled with the complexities of an evolving society and the formidable specter of war. As we look back, the 1910s serve as a vital chapter in the story of the 20th century, a period that shaped the course of history and left an enduring legacy.

ROARING TWENTIES

Roaring Twenties

The 1920s, often referred to as the Roaring Twenties, was a decade of unparalleled cultural change, economic dynamism, and social revolution. It was a time when the world emerged from the darkness of World War I and embarked on a new chapter characterized by exuberance, innovation, and rebellion.

The Jazz Age:
The 1920s is perhaps best known as the Jazz Age, a period marked by the electrifying rhythms of jazz music. This new musical genre, with its roots in African and European traditions, captured the spirit of the era. Jazz legends like Louis Armstrong, Duke Ellington, and Bessie Smith became household names, and the frenetic dance moves of the Charleston and the Black Bottom epitomized the age.

Prohibition and Speakeasies:
Prohibition, the nationwide ban on the sale and consumption of alcohol, fueled a wave of rebellion. Speakeasies, underground clubs that secretly served liquor, flourished. Gangsters like Al Capone and bootleggers became infamous figures in American folklore, while the demand for illicit booze seemed insatiable.

Women's Liberation:
The 1920s brought significant changes to women's lives. The ratification of the 19th Amendment in 1920 granted women the right to vote in the United States. This era also witnessed the emergence of the "flapper," a new kind of woman who embraced short skirts, bobbed hair, and a liberated attitude.

The Age of Innovation:
The 1920s was an age of remarkable innovation. Radio became a dominant form of entertainment, bringing news, music, and stories into people's homes. The first transatlantic flight, made by Charles Lindbergh in 1927, captured the world's imagination. Henry Ford's assembly line made cars more affordable, revolutionizing transportation.

Cultural Icons:
The era was defined by cultural icons like Charlie Chaplin, whose silent films charmed audiences, and Babe Ruth, the baseball legend. New art movements like Art Deco brought elegance and style to design, while authors like F. Scott Fitzgerald and Ernest Hemingway explored themes of disillusionment and the Lost Generation.

Economic Prosperity and the Stock Market:
The 1920s was a time of unprecedented economic growth in the United States. The stock market soared, and many Americans enjoyed newfound prosperity. However, this economic exuberance would come to a crashing halt with the Wall Street Crash of 1929, signaling the onset of the Great Depression.

The End of an Era:
The Roaring Twenties, with its freewheeling spirit and cultural dynamism, was a fleeting moment of revelry before the challenges of the 1930s. The Wall Street Crash and the ensuing Great Depression marked the end of the era of prosperity, and the world would soon be thrust into the turmoil of World War II.

1950S & 1960S

1950s & 1960s

The 1950s and 1960s were a tale of two distinct decades. The '50s represented stability and prosperity, while the '60s were an era of revolution and rebellion.

The 1950s
Economic Prosperity: The 1950s were marked by economic growth and stability. The aftermath of World War II ushered in a period of unparalleled prosperity in the United States and much of the Western world. The GI Bill provided veterans with access to education and housing, while the baby boom brought a surge in population.

The Rise of Suburbia: Suburban living became the idealized American dream. Families moved to the suburbs in droves, and the concept of "keeping up with the Joneses" became ingrained in the American psyche.

Rock 'n' Roll: The 1950s witnessed the birth of rock 'n' roll, a genre that would forever change the musical landscape. Icons like Elvis Presley, Chuck Berry, and Little Richard brought electrifying music to teenagers and initiated a cultural shift. The music was a celebration of youth, rebellion, and freedom.

Television Boom: The 1950s were also the golden age of television. Shows like "I Love Lucy," "The Honeymooners," and "The Ed Sullivan Show" became cultural touchstones. Television became the primary medium for news, entertainment, and advertising, shaping American culture and family life.

The Cold War and Civil Rights: The Cold War tensions between the United States and the Soviet Union defined much of the era. The period was marked by McCarthyism and the Red Scare, with allegations of communist infiltration in American society. Concurrently, the Civil Rights Movement gained momentum as activists fought for racial equality and an end to segregation.

The 1960s
Civil Rights Triumphs: The landmark Civil Rights Act of 1964 and the Voting Rights Act of 1965 ended legal segregation and discrimination, heralding a new era for racial equality.

Counterculture and Rebellion: The 1960s was a decade of rebellion and change. The counterculture movement, driven by youth disillusioned with mainstream society, blossomed. The protest against the Vietnam War and the quest for civil rights defined the era. Iconic moments like the Woodstock Festival in 1969 symbolized the spirit of peace and love.

Space Race and Innovation: The 1960s marked a new frontier in human exploration. In 1961, Yuri Gagarin became the first human in space, and in 1969, Neil Armstrong set foot on the moon during the Apollo 11 mission, signaling America's victory in the Space Race.

Political Assassinations: The era was marred by political assassinations that shook the world. John F. Kennedy's assassination in 1963, followed by Malcolm X, Martin Luther King Jr., and Robert F. Kennedy's murders, were tragic events that cast a long shadow over the decade.

1970S

1970s

The 1970s, often described as the "Me Decade," was a time of profound change, cultural shifts, and unforgettable moments that left an indelible mark on history. From disco balls to bell-bottoms, the '70s embodied a unique blend of rebellion and creativity that defined the era.

The Vietnam War and Counterculture:
The early '70s were marked by the tumultuous end of the Vietnam War. The conflict had divided the nation, sparking anti-war protests and the anti-establishment sentiment of the counterculture movement. Hippies, known for their free-spirited ideals, anti-war stance, and tie-dyed attire, challenged traditional norms.

Disco Fever:
The mid-'70s saw the rise of disco, a genre that set dance floors ablaze. The Bee Gees, Donna Summer, and KC and the Sunshine Band produced the catchy tunes that became anthems for a generation. The disco ball became a symbol of the era's hedonistic nightlife.

Women's Liberation:
The '70s was a time of significant strides for women's liberation. The feminist movement gained momentum, with iconic moments like the women's liberation march in 1970 and the publication of "Our Bodies, Ourselves" in 1971. Women demanded equal rights and reproductive freedom.

Fashion and Pop Culture:
The '70s brought some of the most memorable fashion trends, from bell-bottom pants to platform shoes, maxi dresses to hot pants. People embraced vibrant patterns and colors, often accompanied by oversized collars. Iconic TV shows like "Charlie's Angels" and "The Brady Bunch" reflected the fashion of the times.

Iconic Music:
The '70s was a golden era for music. Rock legends like Led Zeppelin, Pink Floyd, and The Rolling Stones continued to dominate the scene. Singer-songwriters like Elton John, Billy Joel, and Joni Mitchell produced enduring classics. The punk movement, with bands like The Ramones and The Sex Pistols, challenged the musical establishment.

Cultural Moments:
The decade delivered unforgettable cultural moments. "Star Wars" revolutionized cinema in 1977, becoming a cultural phenomenon. The birth of video games with Atari and the release of the first cell phone marked the dawn of the digital age. Disco's influence extended beyond music, infiltrating fashion and dance.

Political Upheaval:
The '70s was marked by political upheaval. The Watergate scandal led to President Richard Nixon's resignation in 1974, casting a shadow over American politics. The Iranian Revolution of 1979 and the subsequent Iran hostage crisis gripped the world.

1980S

1980s

The 1980s, often dubbed the "Decade of Decadence," was a time of excess, exuberance, and innovation. With its bold fashion, iconic music, and technological advancements, the '80s marked a unique period in history that continues to captivate our collective imagination.

Reaganomics and Economic Boom:
The '80s were marked by the economic policies of President Ronald Reagan. His approach, known as "Reaganomics," aimed to reduce government intervention in the economy. Tax cuts and deregulation spurred economic growth, leading to a decade of unparalleled prosperity.

The Rise of Technology:
The '80s saw the rise of personal computers. IBM's PC, released in 1981, revolutionized the way people worked and connected. Meanwhile, the invention of the World Wide Web in 1989 paved the way for the digital age. The Walkman made music portable, and video games like Pac-Man and Super Mario captured the imagination.

Fashion Extravaganza:
Fashion in the '80s was a riot of color, fabric, and flair. Shoulder pads, leg warmers, and acid-washed jeans were all the rage. People flaunted neon hues and bold patterns, often accompanied by oversized belts and statement jewelry. The "power suit" became a symbol of women's increasing influence in the workplace.

The Music Revolution:
The '80s was a musical playground that produced icons like Michael Jackson, Madonna, and Prince. The advent of MTV in 1981 brought music videos into the mainstream, changing how music was consumed. The emergence of hip-hop and rap, with artists like Run-DMC and Grandmaster Flash, reshaped the music landscape.

The Blockbuster Era:
The '80s was the golden age of blockbusters. Movies like "E.T. the Extra-Terrestrial," "Star Wars: The Empire Strikes Back," and "Indiana Jones: Raiders of the Lost Ark" became cultural phenomena. The era of the action hero was born, with stars like Arnold Schwarzenegger and Sylvester Stallone dominating the big screen.

Cultural Phenomena:
The '80s introduced the world to the Rubik's Cube, Cabbage Patch Kids, and the first home video game console, the Atari 2600. Iconic TV shows like "The Cosby Show," "The A-Team," and "Dallas" captivated audiences.

Political Shifts:
The '80s had its share of political shifts. The fall of the Berlin Wall in 1989 marked the beginning of the end of the Cold War. The decade was also marked by the AIDS crisis, prompting calls for awareness and research.

FUTURE

Future

In the not-so-distant future, humanity stands on the precipice of remarkable change. As we look ahead, we see a world where robots, space travel, and biomedicine have revolutionized our existence, propelling us into an era of astonishing possibilities.

Robotics:
Robots are no longer mere machines; they've become integral members of our society. Advanced artificial intelligence (AI) and robotics have given rise to a new generation of autonomous, sentient machines. These robots, capable of learning, adapting, and empathizing, have transformed our workforce, taking on mundane and dangerous tasks. As a result, humans are free to pursue more creative and fulfilling endeavors.

Space Travel:
Space is no longer the final frontier; it's the canvas of our aspirations. The dream of interstellar travel has become a reality. Space agencies, corporations, and even private citizens now explore the cosmos. Colonies on Mars and the moon serve as hubs for scientific research and tourism. Exoplanets beckon as potential new homes, and propulsion technologies have shattered the limits of our cosmic exploration.

Biomedicine:
Biomedicine has undergone a revolution of extraordinary proportions. Genetic engineering has unlocked the secrets of our DNA, eradicating hereditary diseases and enabling human enhancement. We have not only extended our lifespan but also improved our quality of life. Nanotechnology plays a pivotal role in medicine, enabling precision treatments and therapies at the cellular level. We are on the cusp of eradicating diseases once thought incurable.

Energy and Sustainability:
Our approach to energy and sustainability has drastically transformed. Clean, renewable energy sources power our world, making fossil fuels relics of the past. A global commitment to sustainability has revitalized our environment, with reforested lands and revived ecosystems. We've harnessed fusion energy, offering virtually limitless power while minimizing waste.

Global Unity:
The challenges we face have forged a new era of global unity. Geopolitical conflicts have given way to collaborations for the common good. International space agencies pool resources for ambitious exploration missions, and countries work together to combat global threats like climate change and pandemics. In the spirit of cooperation, humanity has found its true strength.

Cultural Fusion:
Cultural fusion has reshaped our world. The blending of traditions, languages, and ideas has given rise to a global culture rich in diversity and inclusivity. Virtual reality and augmented reality have redefined the way we experience art, travel, and education. With access to the world's cultures at our fingertips, we're more interconnected than ever.

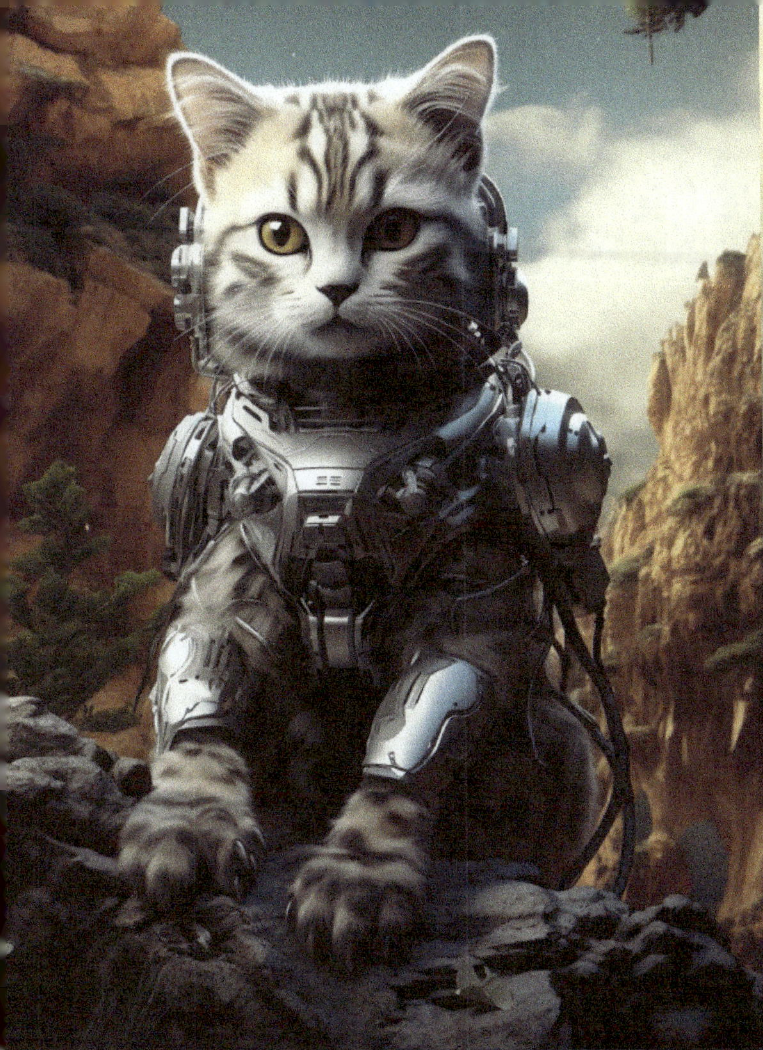
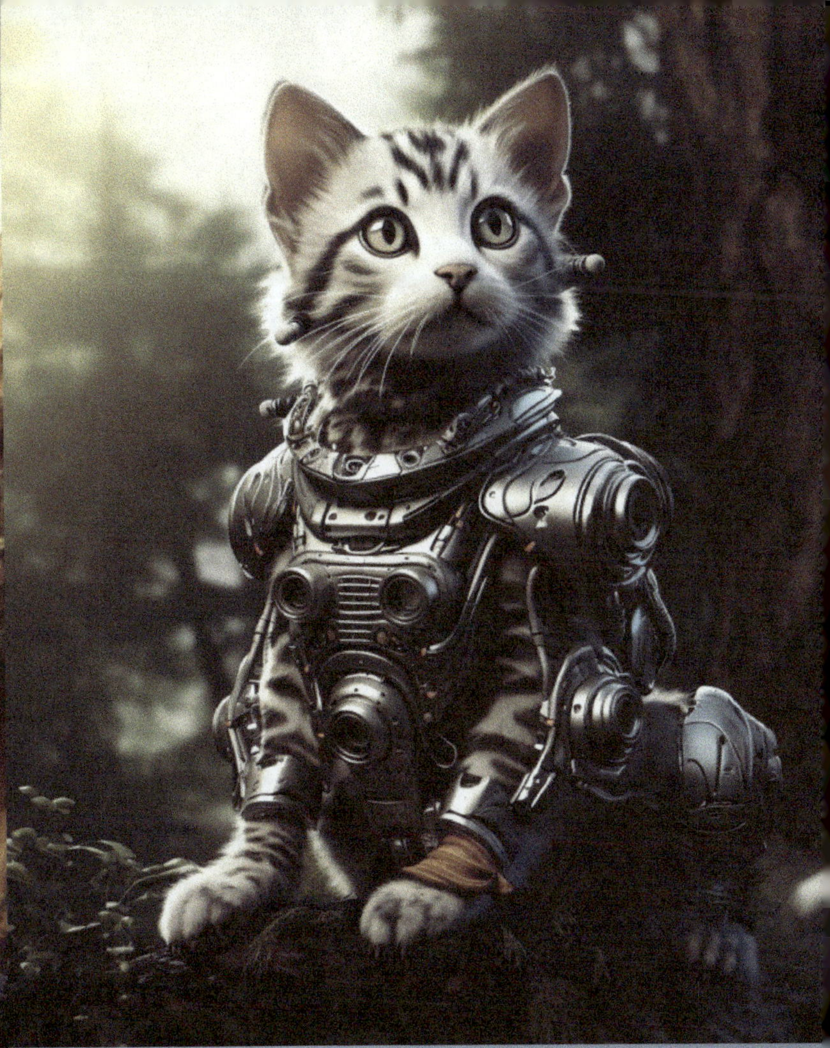
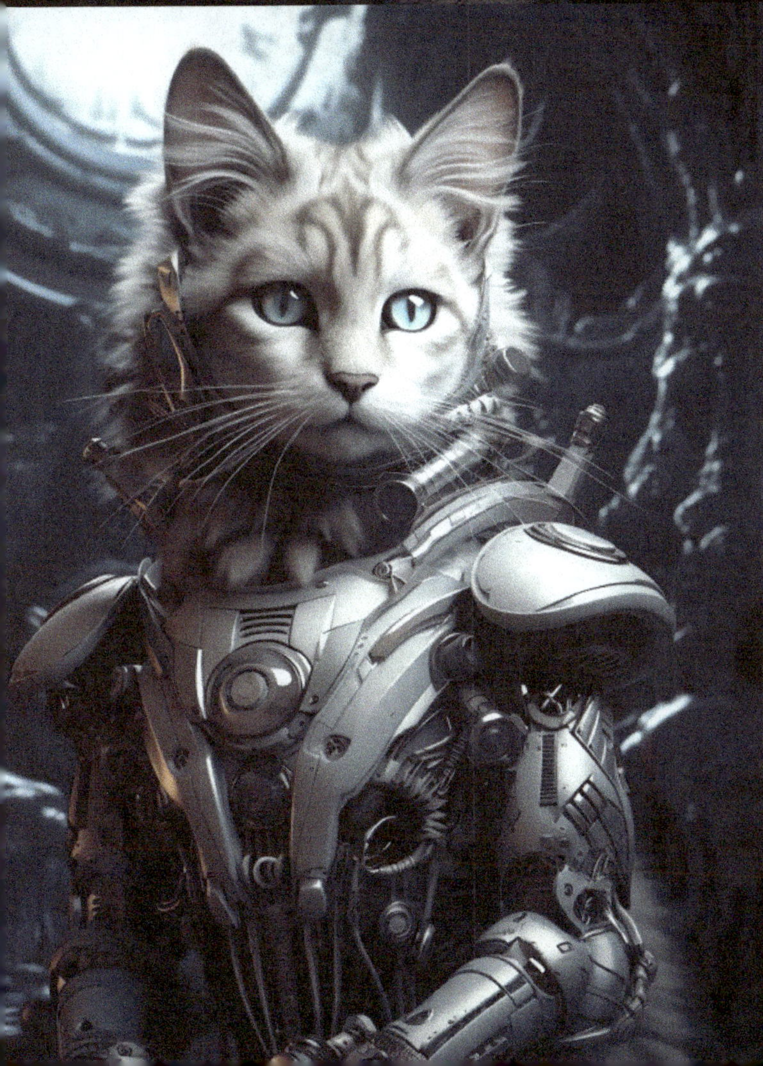
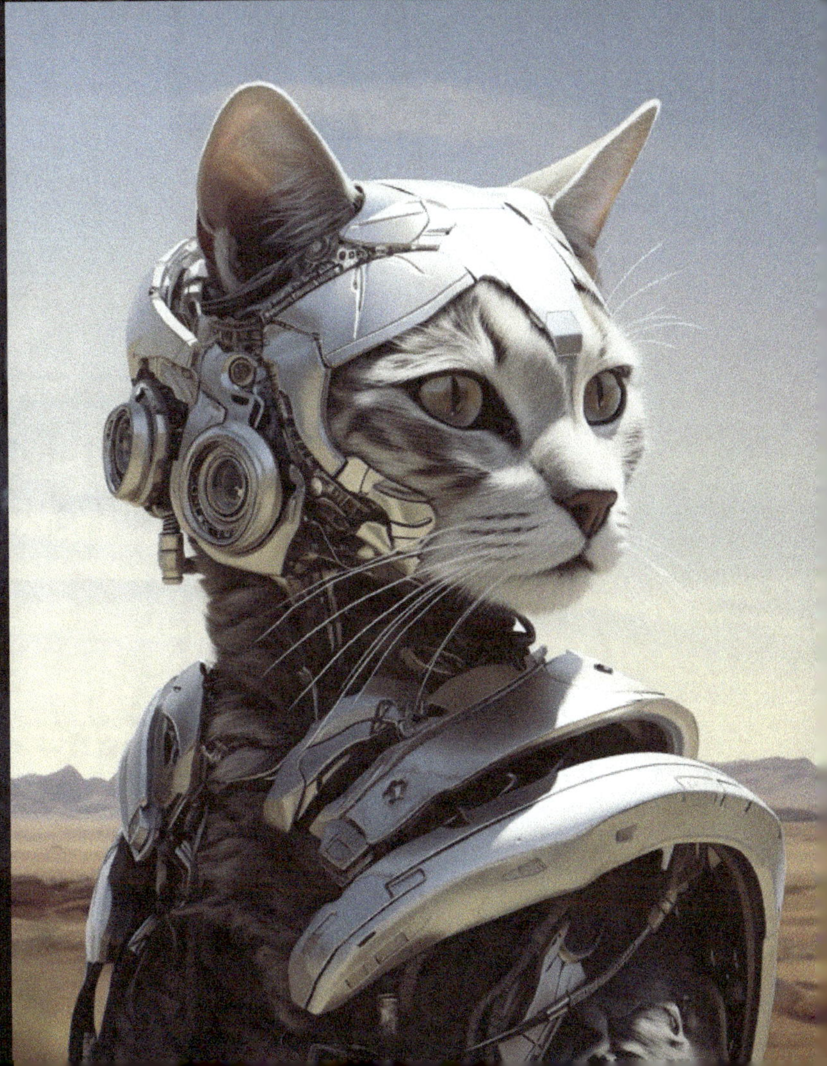

Also by S.C. Francis

Personal Note
If you enjoyed this book, it would mean the world to me if you'd leave a quick, simple review or rating on Amazon, Goodreads, or another site where you purchased it. It helps others find my books and motivates me to keep writing. Thanks for your support.
-S.C. Francis

The Ultimate Book of Fun Things to Do in Retirement Volume 1
Hundreds of ideas to spark your imagination for planning an exciting, active, happy, healthy, and mentally sharp life after work.

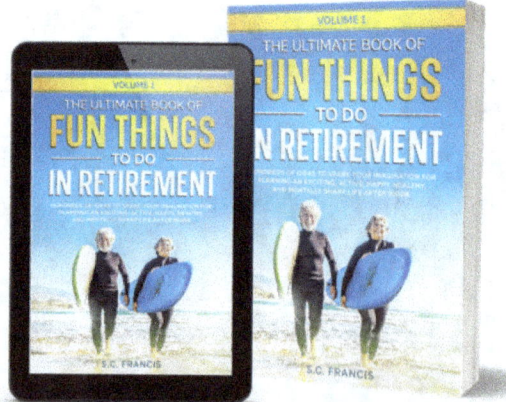 

Pick up Volume 1 on Amazon by scanning the above QR code.

The Ultimate Book of Fun Things to Do in Retirement Volume 2

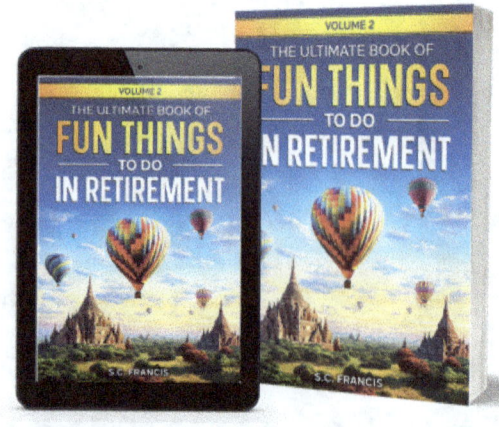 

Pick up Volume 2 on Amazon by scanning the above QR code.